CAMDEN VOICES
1978-90

> For every man whose soul is not a clod
> hath visions, and would speak, if he had loved,
> and been well nurtured in his mother tongue.
>
> **KEATS**

KATABASIS

First published 1990 by Katabasis,
10 St Martins Close, London NW1 0HR

Copyright remains with the authors 1990.

Cover drawing of Inverness St market, Camden Town by John Cook
Designed and typeset by Boldface, London EC1, 01-253 2014
Printed by Short Run Press, 0296 631075
Distributed by Central Books,
14 The Leathermarket, London SE1 3ER, 01-407 5447

ISBN 0 904872 14 9

CAMDEN VOICES
1978-90

An anthology edited by Dinah Livingstone

ACKNOWLEDGEMENTS

Some of these poems have appeared in the following journals and collections:

'Convent Meal': *The Rialto*; 'Boogie Woogie': *The Times Literary Supplement*; 'Zelda Fitzgerald Practising Ballet' and 'Getting the Electricity On': *Passengers to the City* (Hale and Iremonger 1985); 'Amnesia', 'Joy', 'Nawroz' and 'Performance': *Witness to Magic* (Hearing Eye 1989); 'Cleanliness': A *Fistful of Yellow Hope* (Littlewood Press 1984); 'At the Gates': *Cobweb*; 'To My Camden Poetry Group' and 'Chorus': *Saving Grace* (Rivelin Grapheme 1987).

Katabasis is grateful for the assistance of Greater London Arts.

CONTENTS

Preface by William Blake		4
Introduction		5
Prologue	To My Camden Poetry Group	9
Cicely Herbert	Picture of a Far Place	10
	Finding Words	11
	Blue Bathroom	12
	An Encounter with Rembrandt	13
	Spring 1986	14
	On Earth	15
Dennis Simmons	Eagerness	16
	Not On	17
	Babbling	18
Donie Dempsey	Found	19
Elen N.A. Read	Ariadne	20
Veronica Cohen	In the Pink	21
Andrew Woodward	Death	22
	Rumour	23
Steve Doyle	The Clown	24
Shelah Florey	Apéritif	25
	The Messenger	26
	Animals	27
	Phone Call	28
	Video	29
	Afternoon	30
	Solo Dancer	31
Katherine Gallagher	Zelda Fitzgerald Practising Ballet	32
	Getting the Electricity On	33
Jill Bamber	The Dream Tent	34
Zoë Bailey	Ways of Being: Woody	35
Betty Wall	The Moorhen	36
	Five Vignettes of Summer 1979	37
	The Falklands War, May 1982	38

Christopher Truman	Maritime Nation:	
	The Sinking of the Belgrano	39
	Silesia over Dinner	40
	Early Dusk	43
Beate Lux Smeed	Soldier Ghost	44
Francis Oeser	Graffiti	45
John Cook	An Old Man in Camden Town	46
	Sonnet	48
Bob Rodgers	Room to Move Inn	49
Bryan Abraham	L'Invitation au Voyage	50
	Sonnet for Lorraine (Noch!)	51
Elizabeth Trew	Convent Meal	52
Jane Duran	Boogie Woogie	54
	Mating Calls	55
	The Wonderful Belly Dance of Rabah Saïd	56
Susan Jankowski	The Dance	58
	Unselved	59
Zanna Beswick	Heavy Goods	60
Alison Islin	The Harassed Mother	61
Myra Schneider	Cleanliness	62
Mary Mohan	Breakfast in Bed	64
Francesca Reynolds	Hedgehog	65
	Nobody Special	66
	'The Bell' Kings Cross	68
	Five in the Afternoon	69
Jeni	Breaking the Pattern	70
	I Have a Brother	71
David Schiff	Still Experiencing	72
	Nuclear Vision	73
John Jolliffe	Dark Hour	74
Helen Barrett	End of Term: Bar	75
Tim Sanders	November	76
Richard Armstrong	Blue Victoria	77
Mimi Khalvati	Jasmine	78
	The Woman in the Wall	79
	The Cellar	80

Contents

John Rety	Memo: Please Look into This	82
	Declaration	84
Patrick Fetherston	Wanting	85
	Branwell Brontë	86
	An Instant of Deprivation	87
	The Answer is a Very Old Flagstone	88
Roselyn Walter	Words	89
	Rivulet	90
Valerie Chazan	Waterways	91
Dinah Livingstone	Thirst	92
	At the Gates	94
Kathleen McPhilemy	The Mothers' Lament for the Death of Cuchullain	96
	My Formidable Great Aunt	98
	Amnesia	100
	Joy	101
	Nawroz: Kurdish New Year 21.3.1985	102
	Performance	103
Peter Campbell	As the Hazel Burns	104
	Health Act	106
	Fourth Station	108
	Video War	110
	The Pain of Love	111
Brian Docherty	Harlequin and Juliet	112
	Cuts in the Welfare State	113
	The Greatest Violence is Saying Goodbye	114
	The Lizards of Pompeii	115
	Sunday Concert in Noel Park	116
Epilogue	Chorus	117

PREFACE
BY WILLIAM BLAKE

I wander through each chartered street,
near where the chartered Thames does flow
and mark in every face I meet
marks of weakness, marks of woe.[1]

★

The fields from Islington to Marybone,
to Primrose Hill and Saint John's Wood,
were builded over with pillars of gold,
and there Jerusalem's pillars stood.

Pancras and Kentish Town repose
among her golden pillars high,
among her golden arches which
shine upon the starry sky.

The Jew's-harp-house and the Green Man,
the ponds where boys to bathe delight,
the fields of cows by Willan's farm
shine in Jerusalem's pleasant sight...

Is this thy soft Family-Love,
thy cruel patriarchal pride,
planting thy Family alone,
destroying all the world beside?...

In my exchanges every land
shall walk, and mine in every land,
mutual shall build Jerusalem,
both heart in heart and hand in hand.[2]

---

1. From *London*. 2. From *Jerusalem*.

INTRODUCTION

This anthology is a selection of poems produced over the last twelve years by the Camden Voices poetry group, which has met regularly on Mondays in term at the Haverstock Branch of Camden Adult Education Institute.

This Thatcher-dominated decade has seen the destruction of the GLC, the democratic government of London, and now of its former subsidiary body, the Inner London Education Authority, which nurtured our group among so many other imaginative, needy and clamouring life forms as befits a great European capital. Groups such as ours exist through faith in human beings and a human city.

The poems in this book speak of some of the effects of Thatcherism, the public spending cuts and harassment of the poor, property speculation and homelessness, the selling off of public assets, private greed and public squalor, deportations, the Falklands War, the miners' strike and the bombing of Libya by US planes taking off from East Anglia.

The political is not separate from the personal; we experience both as part of one life, the only one we have. These poems also speak of many kinds of love and its delight and difficulties, town and country, the natural world, children, old age, a large variety of characters and their behaviour, betrayals, celebrations, dancing, funny things that happened, memories, hopes, in short the daily and the imaginative life of a broad cross-section of Londoners during the eighties.

This editor has run the group since it started in 1978 and although of course members are free to disagree with me about poetry or anything else(!), it may be worth saying briefly what I like, which has obviously influenced my choice of poems. I am passionately fond of the sound of the spoken language in each individual voice. I believe these sounds are the primary material of poetry and one of the signs of a good poem is that even when you read it silently, you can hear a clear speaking voice and the actual sounds attract you. Listening to poetry, either spoken aloud or read silently, is a skill which highly 'litcrary' critics apparently often lack and one we try to cultivate week after week in the group. I also want this speaking voice to have something substantial to say, so that the serious poet in time produces a recognisable body of work that is consistent, sustaining and generous.

Another mark of a good poem is economy, that it conveys a lot in a little, primarily through the senses, though also, of course, ideas. Within this requirement of concision (for our daily conversations are full of redundancies) I believe poems should be made of the language we speak and to be spoken, a bodily and social act. As Hopkins writes, 'Poetry, the darling child of speech, of lips, and spoken utterance: it must be spoken; till it is spoken it is not performed, it does not perform, it is not itself.' Which of course does not require a poem to be reduced to a mere 'performance poem', whose meaning can be exhausted at one hearing. This 'pedantic boring cry' expressing fear and loathing of a poem's physicality has deep historical roots in a gnostic elitism, in which hatred of the body (especially female) marches together with hatred of the body politic, the people.

But, well trained in theology, Hopkins believes one and the same incarnate word has two natures. So he continues: 'Neither do I mean my verse to be recited only. True poetry must be studied.' A poem must be as complex and intricate as what it wishes to say and the virtue of print is that we can return again and again to a poem that has impressed us. Complexity is part of poetic economy; wilful obscurity is an indulgence practised by arrogant obfuscating aesthetes, often as a cloak for their triviality.

During the decade there have been many poetry 'venues' in London and two particular models can be noted: one corresponding to the Government's market ideology with a dodgy 'elitist' underpinning, and the other more popular. London is a body politic and its spirit, though repeatedly squashed by reactionary central governments, has variously and persistently informed its citizens, even long before it was a County Council. Recently in the last years of the GLC this spirit had a strong celebratory element of social joy, seeking a legitimate London pride, typically, the name of both a strong beer and a tiny flower.

An example of the market-model is the Poetry Society, where an official told me: 'Things have changed here: we don't just put on readings now, we do promotions.' (Let us hope matters may improve.) The second sort of venue is typified by Torriano Meeting House, which puts on free readings by many different poets, including some in foreign languages, at which poets from the floor also read work ranging from the very slight to the excellent. Poets are expected to listen to each other, an essential part of the poetic life of a culture! At a reading in November 1989 to protest against the sale of our water, this editor was privileged to be the guest poet invited to perform a prepared set and anyone else who wished read poems about water. Each single voice added something to the occasion, which became a passionate whole, a sort of water liturgy. With events like these, Torriano functions as a 'poetic base community', with more than enough good poetry to make a recent shrill-voiced 'post-feminist' dismissal of those who frequent such venues as 'talentless politicoes' a Wapping lie. One cannot help smiling at the thought of such a description applied to John Heath-Stubbs, who has often read at Torriano. Many contributors to this book often also read there and we leave the reader to judge whether such snooty abuse bears any discernible relation to their work.

One of the first acts of Ernesto Cardenal when he became Minister of Culture after the Nicaraguan Revolution of 1979 was to set up poetry workshops all over the country. He issued some guidelines for writing poetry, shocking a 'literary mafia' with his first sentence: 'Writing good poetry is easy and the rules for doing so are few and simple.' He then goes on to caution against archaism, thumping rhymes and meters, 'poetic' diction, cliché and verbosity. He advises the use of particular rather than general terms, e.g. 'iguana' rather than 'animal', and proper names. Rather than on ideas poetry should be based on things that reach us through our senses. We should write as we speak with the natural plainness of the spoken language and at the same time try to condense the language as much as possible; all words which are not absolutely necessary should be left out. We discussed these guidelines in our group and apart from some particularly Nicaraguan matters (e.g. the advice to use the more colloquial 'vos' rather than 'tu' for 'you') and a touch of exotic bossiness, we found them useful and often familiar.

Camden Voices is a group where people can try out their poetic voice and develop it. To guard against narcissism and to become acquainted with the best contemporary poetry we can find, the first hour of every meeting is always spent listening to and discussing a few poems by a different, usually twentieth century poet, before going on to discuss member's own work. Many poems have been produced since 1978 and

I hope this selection gives an idea of their vigorous variety. The group has consisted of men and women from many different backgrounds and of all ages. The difference in talent and competence has also been great but the potential has usually been greater still.

When we attend Monday after Monday as audience or even midwives at the birth of each other's poems, this creates a bond, just as when you hear a superb poem performed with that power that Lorca called the 'duende', you may burn, you may feel like crying out and part of what you feel is love. Every poet, however humble, makes the word, and when a poem works because it moves us as beautiful and true, connects us as human beings, when (as in that paradigm of humanity, the theology of the trinity) word flows into spirit, love, it is building the city.

Our city, to which many of us are very attached, is London with its disgraceful extremes of wealth and poverty, its government destroyed, its homeless, its public transport a sick joke. This is the city whose evils Blake condemned and still would today but also the city where he saw the shining pillars of Jerusalem. In his *Oracle concerning Managua*, Ernesto Cardenal, describes this vision as the 'city where each individual finally meets every other, city of found identity and fullness of being together, city of communion.'

We hope our poetic activities over the past twelve years in the inner London Borough of Camden and now this common book of more than forty individual voices may be a modest contribution to that city of communion, 'both heart in heart and hand in hand'.

Dinah Livingstone
Christmas 1989

PROLOGUE

By the Editor

TO MY CAMDEN POETRY GROUP

Yes, I am nasty, I admit you're right,
I get bad tempered at poor quality,
I hurt when I'm impatient for delight,
please take account of human frailty.
But now that powers of darkness threaten doom,
let me salute each individual voice
stuttering for utterance in this tatty room:
we are the living, come let us rejoice.
For if this Christmas here a child is born
in bare simplicity, its name is Hope,
who will have many mothers, not just one
madonna, fathers too, since god can't cope.
We are, we make the word and hence may love;
there is no other trinity above.

Cicely Herbert

PICTURE OF A FAR PLACE

The forgotten city leaps from the waters
walled and complete
an archaeologist's first vision
unaltered by discovery.
I visited this place before my birth.

A traveller, always at sea, shading
sun-dazed eyes from fearful heat
time after time, I'd crane my brain
in search of something inside the city,
half remembered, already understood.

Now, words glide through the still sky
like strange exotic birds
with messages I can't yet quite decipher;
truth defies translation
(scholars' precise displacement of language).

A traveller must navigate the route
by following a simple self-drawn chart;
the meaning found will flame, shine out,
illuminate like evening sunlight
that ignites a single distant dome.

Cicely Herbert

FINDING WORDS

                When I was four
Granny told me flowers
named me intricate floral riddles
wove cow parsley into cowslip tales
and scattered the wild subterranean garlic
that pierced my dog-rose bed.

                At ten years old
like a secret drinker who longs
only for solitude, for the consummation,
the holy fire, the illuminating
the exterminating gulp,
I'd lurk, impatient with company
willing the door's slam, the receding steps,
welcoming silence, chasing the first chaste embrace
of my brand-new, banned
new Enid Blyton book.

                And adult
I cruised the crafted pond of printed page
to seek release in verse's tightening vice
to sound with words the source of unplumbed rage
to gouge the silt with language's device.
Like underwater divers then, who drown
I sucked the life from fuller tanks than mine;
unweighted now, I plunge and corkscrew down
discarding flippers, mask and rescue line.
Perhaps I'm lost and won't return, won't dare
to burst the surface of that private pool
but if I do then I shall grab the air
and learn to shout and sing and play the fool.
Sweet sensual sounds of poetry delight
those dark explorers who discover light.

BLUE BATHROOM

The bathroom steams still
jungle-like
strangely uninhabited.
There's a space here
on the crumpled mat,
an empty place where you were.

The greasy rim's all that remains
of the skin you shed
of dirt you discarded.
Your flannel, draped over the bath
drips drops like tears.
The soap smells of you;
your hair clogs the basin
your toothbrush grins from the mug
the powder you spilt
litters the floor.

The streaming mirror reflects only
my helpless inaction.
The defective shower hangs
useless and abandoned.
It's too late to call a plumber in
too late now to organise a spring-clean
we're all washed up, my bathroom and I.
You've moved on.
You're making a splash
in someone else's tub.

AN ENCOUNTER WITH REMBRANDT

Out walking, not a mile from home
I met old Rembrandt face to face
(a most desirable man)
and spoke to him of death.
The attraction lay in his self-knowledge
bitterness behind him, disappointments forgotten
a limitless ease remained on view
welcoming me in.
When I tried to explain who I am
I became so confused
he politely refused my offer to sit for him
saying it seemed his sight had failed.
As we parted
I remembered, quite suddenly,
that the man who'd crated his portrait
(the one I was looking at) and labelled it
'To Kenwood House on Hampstead Heath'
had suffered on the same day
a quite distressing attack of toothache
and had to have four teeth extracted
without an anaesthetic.

I thought later
probably I'd imagined the whole episode.
On the other hand
the man's existence is certain.

SPRING 1986

The longed-for Spring is late to call this year
and numb beneath the icy paths of flight
I shudder fragmentary dreams of fear
as jets thrust upward into star-pierced night.
I dream that snowdrops wither under trees,
that carcasses lie rotting in the street,
that burning skies collapse in churning seas
and love disintegrates in fearful heat.
I dream that hell's a missile bunker store
where Pluto keeps Persephone in chains
and sends abroad declaring he'll have war –
his messengers F1-11 planes.
Last night the killer ravens gained our shore
like migrant birds who touch to earth once more.

ON EARTH

If I can't go to heaven
I shall ask Chagall
to design me a carpet
so beautiful
angels will jostle
for a place on it.

I'll take his painting
to Serbian weavers
who will use natural dyes
to achieve colours I remember
filling a field in Autumn –
the sprouted blue of individual cabbages
yellow anarchy of weeds
and happy poppy red,
bedded in a heavy Suffolk soil.

If I can create some order from this,
a secure border
out of the tangled bramble hedge,
a safe enclosure,
where I can lie
free to find
the changing patterns of the sky

then

I shan't mind staying
here on earth.

Dennis Simmons

EAGERNESS

Recently it was my birthday,
my sister gave me money.

I hurried
fervently
with my acquired
Poets' Manual,
by the rabbit
in the shop front,
the sloven dog
paddling in the wet.
The steam was gone
from my mother's kitchen,
the dinner served out
– except mine.

Dennis Simmons

NOT ON

Our class member arrived late
at evening school
(just after me),
he claimed there was a gunman barring his route,
and was prevented – by Police –
from bringing out his car, in his street.

BUT

my dear Francis, this is too lame.
You must be prepared to go
through Hell AND CROSS-FIRE!
to get to the poetry lesson.
Dinah, our tutor, told me so
and *she* knows.
(YOU would refrain from coming AT ALL if you were
dead, I suppose.)

You must raise your voice to heaven
and charge
shouting Olivier-like poem or prose (even)
so the shootist comprehends
where you stand.

BABBLING

Kebab is a very strange word
to me, I think,
and never mind where it came from,
its literal meaning or beginnings.
To me it sounds like praise and encouragement
like we used to get as children
from a drunkard Teacher.
Also a Vicar perhaps,
one with a bad cold.
'Kebab the good work...'
And likewise, speaking of an old school friend,
'Kebab a nice new bicycle...'
– meaning you admired Keith's two-wheeler.
Being in the Evening Class I'm in
I'm inclined to order Donie Kebab
or Dinah Kebab.

Donie Dempsey

FOUND

'Look at the fascinating
way this opens.'
And he watched
...fascinated
as she opened
her self to him
(the dress falling
to the ground)
as she came
towards him
he entered
into her
love
...and remained
fascinated at the way
she opens
her body to him
(lovingly lovingly)
her mind suffusing
him with light
the mad swirl
of water
over rocks
as they watched
fascinated
love
finding itself
in them.

Elen N.A. Read

ARIADNE

There once was a maiden named Ariadne
who saved her loved Theseus with a thread.
He later forsook her,
this devilishly shook her.
Had she failed in her project? Had she?

Had she foiled him from the unnumbered dead
by cleverly unravelling a spool of thread,
from the gnashing jaws
of the fierce Minotaur
only to boost him for another's bed?

Poor Ariadne! Had she? Had she?
Had she failed? How she paled!
How she wished she were dead!
She steadfastly held the valued view
that marriage vows are sacred.

Veronica Cohen

IN THE PINK

Imagine – if you will –
Barbara Cartland lying dead and still
in a coffin made of pink
and lined in pleated silk.

Her eyelashes fixed with glue
for the last time
brush her cheeks,
which have in their turn been brushed
with pink powder.
Her dress, her hat and finally
at her feet her dog, a peke,
have all been dyed to match.

Andrew Woodward

DEATH

Switching off the telly,
you fade to a small dot.
Your brain leaks energy,
you open your mouth to speak,
nothing comes out.

MAYBE THIS IS IT.

People ignore you,
pretend you're not there
and so, you're not –
Banished to Coventry,
popular consensus decides
you no longer exist –
Too small to register as anything,
a blip on a tv screen,
a dream the size of an ant,
whoever you are –
nobody's interested.
You're so different now,
we call you DEAD.

RUMOUR

In medieval times,
when Rumour was King,
people spread the news by gossiping:
'Noon was the blackest hour
when a three-headed child was born,
fathered by a priest!
Blood was its food,
and strange was its tongue.'

Now in the modern manner,
we debate the Facts:
'A plague has come from Africa,
terrible is its power and many are the dead.'
Like Chinese whispers,
each adds their own lie:
'You can get it by shaking hands.'

The three-tongued media dragon
furnishes our bare imaginations:
'It always snows in Russia,
that's why oranges cost ten pounds each.'
And so the lies are spread to every corner,
so we can hold our noses and say:
'I'm glad I didn't live then!'

Steve Doyle

THE CLOWN

I tear my arms off
one by one
left with two
off balance
I fall forward occasionally
I bleed a little from the nose

The maniac is loose with a gun, I'm told
heroes not needed
where are my arms?
Rain washed them away

I see a red nose underneath my eyes
I challenge the audience
they only look the same as yesterday

Someone has stolen my coloured arms
leaving red holes
someone is waiting with a gun
someone is always waiting with a gun

The audience applaud
the clown undresses
pulls ribbons from his scars
removes a red nose
revealing a red nose
sings to the holes where his arms were
the maniac bursts in
and shoots
the maniac hates singing.

Shelah Florey

APÉRITIF

She shook like a drink,
danced her liquid way
under the lights.
How careful they were the men
ringing her round – like connoisseurs
keeping their distance,
taking time.
Still she was gone
and down their throat
died quickly,
leaving only
the drained colour of her skin.

THE MESSENGER

He was never a one for taking part,
he carried other people's words
and stood by waiting
for mysterious replies –
he thought their activity was wonderful.

At school he didn't understand,
sat by the window on his own,
never a high flyer.
Until he got a job as messenger
and took off with Mercurial wings.

ANIMALS

And certain shapes
come trembling out of space,
stagger up and wander for a while,
in the evening jigsaw the horizon.

Private and unlanguaged stand,
but our eyes meet, I touch one with my hand,
we share blood and something of the land.

PHONE CALL

The public phone
rings ceaselessly
she picks it up
who is that, they ask.

Something sly
a sort of game
what they really
want to know, is there

anyone at all
are they walking
vibrant and so on
reassure themselves.

Maybe they're lost
can't believe
it still goes on
the universe and stuff

a tentacle
they don't want grabbed
who is that?
Just testing really.

VIDEO

He is not here any more
occupying room and floor,
he has gone away.
Yesterday I saw
some strange gesticulating image of him,
mocking, coloured grotesquely.

Marvellous they say
run the tape through
any time you like,
except misted, gently done,
just now I'd have him quiet as a ghost,
only there when he chooses to find me.

AFTERNOON

Partly spent,
partly experienced,
emerging late.

Older skies,
clouds eyebrow raised,
passing what they recognise.

The leaves continuing,
light remembered,
not having to be startled,

to adjust,
to settle,
to be first thing.

Learnt, absorbed,
sunk into things,
met and joined together –

lying and rested,
a live-in lover,
achieved, accepted.

Appreciate, stretch out,
the time seems longer now,
touch it as it passes.

SOLO DANCER

The dancer sets out and does,
she takes action about being,
goes into dangerous space
and makes something unafraid.

Her positive whirl,
arms warding off nullity,
she comes forward and away
from the roots, the safe beginning.

She has something to say with air,
lifts it up and throws it
round her like a shawl,
shapes it from inside.

Becomes mathematical,
stretching the lines out.

The void stands round her
ordered just away,
the blank assembly
waiting its turn
soon to take over
but patient, startled even,

by her sudden leap, her unexpected
look towards it and away,
the closed and moving ring
she has become –
keeping it back,
it has no entry to.

Katherine Gallagher

ZELDA FITZGERALD PRACTISING BALLET

Zelda dances, dances,
weaves her implacable dream:
sometimes it drifts
but her eye snares it in,
the pattern that she counts on
to screen her other face –
glittering flapper-doll
harrying the night.

All that fever and sequins
discarded like an empty day,
past the fret of her marriage –
the book-heroine yoke.
Beside her old zany flights
she has sworn now to dance for real,
to make her own name. *It is not too late.*

Hours lag, skein the day –
she loops and dips, dizzy with steps:
there are no crowds lighting, wrapping her in
but with each wild leap, she parcels fury,
strains for a choreography
to reach her self.

GETTING THE ELECTRICITY ON

The farm has changed, face-lifted
since we put away the lamps
or hung them up with lanterns, as antiques.
The house is new-veined, lush.

Getting the current switched through – such
fever, a district-do to celebrate:
'We'll be like the townsfolk now,' we sang.
My mother saw the world transformed
by a washing-machine and fridge.

My father, caught by progress in a skein
that swept about his ears,
tracked voyages round the farm
reassured by the sameness of the stars
and lanterns lighting his mind.

Jill Bamber

THE DREAM TENT

To Rudi

At first it was hard
to let him into my dream tent
and be invaded.
My bed-channels sloped
with his weight.
I was amazed
to feel the sun warmth
spreading through my spine.
Our limbs flowered outward
from their dual stem,
and the tide of his breath
pulled me like a towed boat
towards sleep.

All day he is gone
wrenched by a tunnel-plunging train,
his shoulders strung with braces,
work-yoked, tender flesh dinted
by diamond criss-cross patterns
of string vest.
I hate the smell of trains
which mean his absence, yet
when he comes home it is hard
to let him into my dream tent.

Zoë Bailey

WAYS OF BEING: WOODY

While we eat macrobiotic beans and rice
tasting each delicate mouthful carefully,
Woody crunches the bones of fresh-killed mice.

While we seek relaxation on the floor,
made comfortable with cushions,
he shows us how,
outstretched on a board, dangling one limp paw.

He is.
He is this cat.
He is himself – to the ends of his whiskers
and the uttermost curve of his claws.

But he licks me.
Lies beside me and licks me,
as if I were cat like him,
massaging me with his tongue,
accepting me with a lick,
as if licking and liking were one.
Then failure, guilt and loss
that bell me with their weight
are lifted, and for those moments,
he is: I am: and we lie together.

Betty Wall

THE MOORHEN

The moorhen
is a lesshen
in economical desighen.

FIVE VIGNETTES OF SUMMER 1979

1

Snow scene in July?
Yes, black poplar's wool explodes,
white and unruly.

2

Fresh-cut sun-baked logs,
the Forestry Commission's
neatly stacked Swiss rolls.

3

A friendly spider
locks my cottage door with web,
after I have gone.

4

Red flag is folded –
dried pepper pot of poppy,
sleep your seeds till spring.

5

Knotted, gnarled and spurred,
the elderly trees hold fast,
claw the ground like fowl.

THE FALKLANDS WAR, MAY 1982

The Sheffield sank this year in spring,
a Falklands' spring in May:
but here the woods were newly dressed
with bluebells' sweet display.

The Ardent fell and Antelope,
in bitter sea-cold war.
Said columbine to celandine:
'I've seen it all before.'

While apple trees and cherries bloomed,
the Coventry had died.
The Pope broke bread in Canterbury:
'Buy poppies for each side.'

Christopher Truman

MARITIME NATION: THE SINKING OF THE BELGRANO

1

Was the ship beyond the exclusion zone,
taunting a stretched administration's wrath,

yet convenient for the submarine
whose log was later ditched by a tow-path?

2

As the gradient of the cruiser's slope –
the pack ice radiant, in sun, further south –

dipped, cringing in the tracking periscope
awash in the closing currents of death

how long did the dim bits stay aired at bottom
before the water pressure pushed as far?

Was the truth, then, jettisoned like jetsam
and to rust deep with the torpedo's scar?

3

Yet: the unloved, hectoring enthusiast,
and the raging dictator in paroxysm,

did they join, divided beneath a common mast?

SILESIA OVER DINNER

For Henryk Szews

Charity from the Vatican,
that encouraged candle-power
up in a dark to resurrect
faith, hope in with Communism

the ploughs now obeying tractors
in teams along the Polish plain
'... once the heart of an Empire
stretching from the Baltic to the Crimea...'

So the Pole in the restaurant,
almost pained in the gorging West
started to extol the future,
endeavour to translate the past.

'... Rolling Silesia is forever.
Do you want to buy a castle
in Poland? Now, prices are low.
You have to buy it off the State,

and undertake to renovate.
Already the black-market rich,
our *nouveau-riche*, are buying them.
I incline to pessimism.

I think we may need them again,
though not for the slaughtered riding
class, who died in the cavalry
beneath the tracks of the Panzers,

or later died climbing Russian
American-built tanks... Poland
is always in the way. Soldiers
from Germany and vast Russia

keep on charging across, warring.
When the Germans came, we hid. When
the Germans had to retreat
and the Russians came, we walked south

into Hungary, starved and hid.
Before that, the Russians rounded
up, and shot, two hundred thousand
of the most notable people

in Poland, my father amongst
them. He could not come south with us.
After this, how can you incline
to optimism? How was it,

that after all this, we just sank
lower? Before the second war,
there was a formal elegance.
In my town, on the clean pavements

there were cafés and restaurants,
couples in fresh sunlight, trees and laughter.
Destroy the brains of a country
and that country may not rise again.

Now... we have be to *given* meat.
And even now, Silesia,
once rich, remains a burning sore.
Our borders were moved further west

by Stalin. Was this a long joke
for history to appreciate?
Germany wants Silesia back,
and western Russia will not budge.

Now, the Bonn–Berlin axis,
with rebuilt industry to match...
our greatest hope is that, next time,
they will buy it, and the Ukraine...'

Silesia, long coveted
by Empress Maria Theresa,
long part of rich southern Prussia,
staked by Prague, turned to Poland on a plate.

The smoke rose in the London restaurant
from the table that had just seen
supplication, a demonstration
for the restraint of all nations.

'... Poland, once an abattoir
itself destined for the graveyard,
a disputed march, sausage waste,
flattened, sandwiched, quartered...'

EARLY DUSK

In an empty room,
the pale autumn sun
warms a calm and whitened
drawing-room wall

as it dips, almost level
to a hedgerow
fifty feet away
in the darkening garden.

Above full plant-trays
light plays on a wall

in paint intent ways.

It is too early
for lights to come on,
and a chair can yet
be moved to the sun

even with twigs in the rays
off the horizon
thrown in relief
on a wall before they come.

From the dying blaze
light falls on a wall

every few days.

Beate Lux Smeed

SOLDIER GHOST

In the savage dark before November dawn
he reappears – my soldier ghost,
his face still boyish after seventy years,
his accusations fresh
as at the instant of his fall.

'Expendable was I – and my generation?
Always more where we came from,
until the best had fought and gone,
while the frail remained – and the generals,
to claim civilisation from a ravaged world.

What happened to the promised fruit
grown from the rose-red seed?
Or the sapling silver birch
rooted with ceremony and my name
into unyielding earth?

Look deep into sun-speckled pools,
find echoes of village children's play.
They are closer to me
than hymns of destiny
or cool men preaching peace.'

Francis Oeser

GRAFFITI

Skill for Inner Peace

Is it a put-up job
by a hungering unemployed
with itching fingers
wishing to better the world?

What secret midnight scrawl –
the Great Idea –
a belief in making,
in building better places
our green land
and so, some happiness;
what rare rich insult
to the usual catchphrases!

But look again!
The 'S' more recent,
fainter, a planted front.
Sign of a loving hand
tired of ugliness and doubt
and the hopeless selfish
messages that flog the brain;
a loving magic 'S'

transforms fragmenting lies
and answers agony's baseness
bends the eye from pavements
to the living sky.

John Cook

AN OLD MAN IN CAMDEN TOWN

Here I sit in my small patch of Camden Town
out of the way and yet so close
to those routes where the traffic goes
to Cambridge and the Fens – to dons and ducks,
or up the Great North Road
past the Nag's Head
pointing to destinations more remote,
trunk routes, motorways and all,
their roar no more than a muffled snore
beyond the houses on York Way.
Good luck to them
taking the noisy crowds away,
taking them all away.
Thank you.

From somewhere underground at intervals
a devil's drum
dumdum! dumdum!
signals that another load of city slaves
is burrowing its way to Potters Bar
or that more ambitious travellers
crowd an Inter-City bullet aimed at places
in the industrial North
or at those foreign parts over the border.
Taking the noisy crowds away,
taking them all away.
Thank you.

Above my head a distant snarl
tells me that packaged crowds
have braved interminal delays,
unfastened safety belts and settled down
to wait for Benidorm, Bermuda or Bombay.
Good luck to them – and to those jumbo jets
taking the noisy crowds away,
taking them all away.
Thank you.

Meanwhile, seated in comfort,
my hands folded behind my head,
I watch the clouds drift idly
between my neighbour's roof
and the garden wall.
I squint the sun
through trellises of green fig leaves
and russet vine,
and while I press the fragrance
from the rosemary
I watch the bees weigh down the flowers
and think:
Why jostle in the crowds
to go to distant places?
I gather my harvest here
and am content to stay
right where I am in Camden Town.

I only ask one thing,
as the Caledonian clock repeats its chime,
to see a friend drop in from time to time.
Thank you.

SONNET

If I should tell my secret love to you,
lament my empty bed, my passion caged,
then might I lose the friendship that I knew
and reap the anger of your youth outraged.
But worse by far would be the cruel fate
if I should gain your tender love and know
that time will soon cut short our happy state
and leave you mourning in my winter's snow.
I would but could not bind your heart to me,
and if I could, I would not risk your tears,
so I must be content to see you free
to fill with joy the springtime of your years.
But oh! from me full seventy years have gone,
and so this sonnet must remain –

Anon.

Bob Rodgers

ROOM TO MOVE INN

If you search around in your heart
you'll find me snug and comfy there.
If you should try to prise me out,
I fear there's something you may tear.
I know I snuck in when you was unaware
but now I'm here don't turn me out,
for you'll be all empty there.
Settle down now you've found me
for it was lonely here.
Together we will win the world
and fill all hearts that care.

Bryan Abraham

L'INVITATION AU VOYAGE

(after Baudelaire)

Cool baby, soul sister,
dig this dreamy sweetness,
dropping out to groove together.
Slow loving, no hurry,
go on loving until dying
someplace deeply you.
Wet-look suns in mist-hazed heavens
magic-charm my soul
with the mysteries
of your lying eyes,
moist and dazzling.
Laid-back land of beauty,
jive-free,
made for hedonistic
sensuality.

SONNET FOR LORRAINE (NOCH!)

Should autumn's auburn evenings spend their hour
or springfresh blossom cease to scent the breeze;
were winter's snowstark landscapes shorn of power
to block my breath with virtuoso's ease;
had Presley never waxed in Memphis sun,
le Carré's Smiley proved to be the mole;
though Guinness burn to acid on my tongue
and Hoddle not crusade for Spanish goals;
were all to crumble that I held secure
and night concuss with day to merge confused,
my senses lacerated to endure
as arid husks discarded and abused;
though all to blackened nothing should succumb,
I'd still get horny picturing your bum.

Elizabeth Trew

CONVENT MEAL

Today
Mother Superior
presides at High Table.
Solid in habitual black she
graces the food,
sits and eyes
tranquilly
whorls of girls in
drifting blue – tender
petals of profusion whose
transient faces
hover above the brisket
eddying high sound
as the water-jug passes.

While she,
over bread pudding
ever smiling,
enquiring,
sinks teeth – smooth ivory notes
vigorously
into the sweet.

Later
we rise to more prayer,
her girls dispersing into hazy sky
of their outside court,
flying fine hair and bones
between the bells.

While she,
highest mother of the house,
swings heavy robes through
hallowed corridors of days,
continuously.

Jane Duran

BOOGIE WOOGIE

Soap edge shoes slip nine ways
in the gymnasium, awake all night.
We have opened the small windows at the top,
goblets of stars in a blur.

The girls, the fellows on the steps.
We discover the night porcupines
in the grass, the slopes of fireflies.
The geranium gymnasium calls us back.
We cannot sleep. We cannot sleep.

We line up along the walls
in blue chiffon, in tucks and frills,
with sad bony shoulders, in pale lemon shoes

we spin out along the polished floor
all the mosquito folly of the dance.

MATING CALLS

Cat call, Tom weather.
He growls in the utmost desire,
leads her to the moonmouse
along the railings,
and his clean Himalaya
white bell silence
is also persuasive
as a cloister
with one orange tree
and calls her to a halt.

Whereas
between leaving
and arriving
your hands along
my ribcage
let in light
through the slats,
and the canary inside
near the pot of geraniums
begins to sing
when you sing.

THE WONDERFUL BELLY DANCE
OF RABAH SAÏD

When Rabah dances
in his tiny apartment
in the centre of Malmö
his friends round the coffee table
witness
his belly imperious.

When he shimmies
between the television set
and the picture window

landmarks surface out of the fog.
At the black docks
the lights of the ferry to Copenhagen
turn on all at once.

He unbuttons his shirt.
He locks his hands behind his head
whirls and shudders on the spot

and the last stars leap
between the branches of fir trees.
Over the fleeting farmlands
barn doors open
to let out their dark.

In sedate parade meanders
the gleam of cattle haunches,
and breath has an edge of snow
an edge of sirocco

like two cusps of the moon
when Rabah lifts up his arms
and laughs down at his dancing belly
over the astonished
rooftops of Malmö

and a young bridegroom, lying awake
remembers a riddle
from his childhood
when Rabah spins down the hallway

gliding, eddying
across the marine snow of Sweden:
a sandstorm at dawn,
his red shirt – banners.

Susan Jankowski

THE DANCE

We are all bursting with something.
Some with love,
you with death,
she with birth.
The fullness swells
and fills and overwhelms.
Drains.

The dance continues.
A circus perhaps.
He taps us on our shins, says:
'Step in time.'
To the tree:
'Grow, blossom, fall.'
To us:
'Die.'

We are full.
Awash with tears.
A fallen beech leaf rustling.
We are the sap,
sticky, yielding
sweet solder of growth.
Fall again.

Damp autumn leaf layers
crushed against the grey wall.
Fecund and soft.
Poor old Michael Finegan,
begin again.

UNSELVED

What do you do?
They ask. I sigh.
Prepare to be pinned down.
Painless category.

They are secure.
I am awash.
No chance to elaborate
change or explain.
The fence encloses the idea
total and forever.

They are free to go now.
Free.
I am unselved.
I can see them
having seen me naked, leave
unperturbed.

I am undone.
I will be silent.
A straight line between my lips
to put off all comers.

Zanna Beswick

HEAVY GOODS

I pour you out of the thermos.
I find you lying between the white
slices of my sandwiches,
whispering over Radio One.

I roll, I roll along the lanes
of the motorway,
slipping between your thighs
stretched under me;
I watch you crawling by the hard shoulder
when I pull out, pull out,
stretch the wheels over the concrete,
wanting you again,
and driving the great bulk.

I don't know how to talk
while you sit in my truck,
how to come back to you
with my oil-stained want choking me.

The tracks on your skin disgust me
where I ran you over,
drove down your resistance,
put you out of gear.
Now I am stuffed with you,
bearing the cargo further and further
over the miles;
and trundling through nights,
petrol-fillings, cups of tea,
all smelling of you
and the ditch I lay you in.

Alison Islin

THE HARASSED MOTHER

Fragile as a new-born star
your face etched in innocence
but oh how that toddler's tongue does hurt
and challenge: 'Mum I dare!'
My hands they tremble
in despair they shake
to such a rage and strike,
though it's rare.

And then your tears as raindrops do
spill in a single trail.
I mop them up and hide my pain
repentant in my shame.
But still you hug me,
forgiven again.

Never again I cry
and cry
until the next time
I sigh.

Myra Schneider

CLEANLINESS

Cleanliness
next to godliness?
To me it's a dirty word
which I'd like to use
to wipe the smiles off all the families
in their whiter than snowy whites,
in their kitten-soft woollens,
eating golden flakes
and sparkling like their kitchens.
Images like these nourish brains
connected to hands forever washing,
forever wringing out the blood.

There's gaunt Mrs Flint
who suffers her husband's patients
to wait in her scoured front room
pinned with tight-lipped notices:
No smoking;
Do not scrape the chairs
against the white-washed walls;
Do not scuff the shampooed carpet
(or soil the air by breathing it!)
Boys with grime-engrained knees and knuckles
set her teeth on edge
for they will surely smear, smudge,
or otherwise contaminate her sacred property.

There's old Mr Skeap
sweeping the immaculate velveteen of his lawn
while his plants stand to symmetric attention.
Every autumn he rants
because frivolous leaves from neighbours' trees
infiltrate his garden and deface it.
There's pinch-cheeked Mrs Purse
crocodile-snapping at her catarrhal child:
Don't kick balls on muddy grass;
Don't touch tins of messy paints,
Never sink your hands in DIRT.

So he perches on the pale floral sofa,
stares listlessly at the box
and when he goes to school runs amuck.
There's subnormal Sandra
indoctrinated so that she will not eat
a digestive biscuit
without swaddling herself
in paper serviettes.

Godliness?
Good God! All this scrubbing,
all this guarding of virgin surfaces,
squeezes out the fun,
blocks brains, chokes joy
while ruby time dribbles out.
Oh yes, this disease is a killer!

Mary Mohan

BREAKFAST IN BED

Waking to the cool mist-blue
of a room I hardly know
I remember how we painted it this colour
when last year's snow
was a thick white crust on the window.

Now everything has melted – the ice
brittle and cutting as the raw shock of words
that snapped between us at the touch
of a hard wind from nowhere,
the shaking cold of love leaving
for the seagulls in the downpour.

Melted to the scent of Juniper
and Tamarisk in bloom, the sun on cotton,
a trickle of yellow splashes through bamboo,
to the aroma of hot rye bread
and dark roast Arabica,
to you now in the doorway, a smile,
cups clinking on the tray.

Francesca Reynolds

HEDGEHOG

Curled up
racked
resentful hedgehog
or knotted snake
ever ready to unravel
and hiss
I glare at the womb
that grips me tight
in a fist of steel
diluting legs
blurring brains
undeterred by threats
or aspirin.

Later
metal melted to velvet
I stretch and purr
call the truce
I know I'll break
in renewed monthly rage
when this strange 'it'
stubbornly reasserting
a will of its own
makes us both animals
locked
in a love-hate zoo.

NOBODY SPECIAL

You are, you always will be
my great unanswered question.
Blank space, faceless,
of an impossible crossword
without the help of clues.
My father
and I wouldn't know you
if you had been the man
I see on the underground
– the one in the dirty overcoat
singing lullabies to a sherry bottle,
or the man at the corner
who asks me the time,
while his eyes, undressing me,
ask for something more.
You are probably nobody special
just a puzzle
I don't even know
why I want to solve
except that one day
early in the sixties
you met my mother, and smiled.
Maybe you had lips like Mick Jagger,
maybe you had teeth like JFK;
maybe you took her to see
the new boys from Liverpool
and asked her to hold your hand.

But where there had been one woman
suddenly there were two
and you wanted no part
in multiplication.
So you left,
man where my maybes
and could-have-beens meet,
for probably no other reason
than that you were
nobody special.

'THE BELL' KINGS CROSS

The serpents have made Eden.
Fallen angels rise in a banshee shower
foam kicked up
from a sea of shifting angles,
jaws and cheek-bones red-lit, green-lit
divine among the night colours.
On the dance floor
Venus high on snakebite
stretches strong black arms
to her black-clad sister.
They leap and sing,
hazy air tears before them.
At the bar
the young god drinks red witch,
watches its sour cloud
swirl and heave in a pint glass
not quite sure
if it's liquor or magic;
doesn't care
because he and the barman
are madly in love.
Madonna's a virgin again
this Saturday night
and the fused rhythms
of a song, a glance,
mix like a cocktail,
intoxicate.

FIVE IN THE AFTERNOON

Your naked look undoes me
button by zip
till, stripped
of clothes and pretensions
we roll over, laughing
at the sheer decadence
of being in bed
at five on a winter violet
afternoon, vermilion-tinged
with the twilight
every city dweller knows:
when it's just dark enough
for skin to smudge like charcoal,
just light enough
for me to see
my own fingers glide and glow
down your milky-way back.
Our resistance is toppling
down this same sweet slow slope.
We know it, watch it
gather languid momentum;
let our stories unwind,
twine together
supple, so easy, we can't stop wanting
to tell them,
breathless,
over and
over.

Jeni

BREAKING THE PATTERN

I keep away,
for I know how easily
I could lose it all,
how little you need do
to make me melt like picnic butter
on a fly-high, sun-soaked day.
But recently I heard
you were still breathing,
still beautiful,
still living in London.

And that was enough.

Away I went
seeping into frost baked wrinkles of winter earth,
my slippery heat forcing sleeping seeds to flower.

I HAVE A BROTHER

And when our father died
he wept
like a large, obdurate rock.

No sound, no movement, all heart
breaking over the cream and brown smoothness
of his eyes.

And all I could do
was hold on to him.

My two hands barely covering his one.

Feeling him crumble
as the glistening grief
left salt-white marks I could not wipe away.

David Schiff

STILL EXPERIENCING

I wonder
respecting that there are many coloured coats
on fish in the sea
how
there are so few colours on our skins

In some passion
caressed eyes
stroked lips

While some flowers have colours
we seem to have shades

Between sleep and wake
tongues touch

Grass can be luscious
streams glisten
bats have voices
shriller than our ear drums
can hear

But we still value ourselves
more than anything
ourselves
as if hands can make up
for all else

NUCLEAR VISION

'Do not watch
stay five miles off';
I lay my head
on the sand
and prayed

In my eyes
as the mist rose
and the yellow glaze
penetrated my body
I saw you

'There is no danger,
just avert your eyes';
I kept them shut
cupped in my hands
and prayed

But the vision of you
hazy yellow in the mist
seemed larger and
deeper than the sound
of fission

And trembling
with love and hate
like small exploding particles
my eyes opened
but I couldn't see

John Jolliffe

DARK HOUR

Red swan gliding silently
through my dreams
lonely soul in hot air-streams
off the edge
and gone forever
too late to touch the heart.

In the darkness
more silent than moths' dust
a tiny glistening child
falls to the ground
and melts into the earth.

The night is quiet.
There is no sound.

Helen Barrett

END OF TERM: BAR

I don't feel at all like going.
Lucy wants it to snow.
But it's not in the realm of snowing,
That I feel I would rather not go.
No.
No, it's not in the realm of snowing,
Though where it's at is a penguin's dip –
Oh, if only I'd met a grey penguin
    with a blue sash around its dim hips
And a swagger within its curve's function
That would teach me to question its tips,
Gently.
Then perhaps in some new realm of being,
If the lamps didn't burn over-bright,
If their glow was quite feeble and smiling,
I could leave here and still feel all right.

Tim Sanders

NOVEMBER

Grey porridge days
dawdle through this month

soil crusts, grass tousles,
trees dance in tatters

a grizzled sky drizzles
sags like a sopping sheet.

We guy ourselves up:
rockets, scarlet paper poppies –

brazen out the interval
between sharp tints and tinsel.

Richard Armstrong

BLUE VICTORIA

Rebecca,
today
all
I wanted
was to spend a
flyscreendoor
summer evening
under a shade tree
with you.

Instead of a
radio-blaring
polaroid heatwave
in the
middle of London
on
my
own.

Mimi Khalvati

JASMINE

if you find
the end of the root
in the scent of jasmine
and bind it through

till your sight
is amnesia
and your breath
love's wound

you will wake with blossoms
starring your hair
the will
to live more sweetly

girdling you
in ebbing rings
like Titania
smiling at an ass

THE WOMAN IN THE WALL

When she turns to her mirror, water sees
her other selves, in other seasons,
the crystal gown she wore to the iceman's ball,
the fractured nebulae of Eve.

Here, too, the grasses spring
from earth that holds the trace, the heel
of pilgrim feet, snatching at the child
who broke away inside the ring, marvelling.

Stonewalling reaffirms an older faith
we had as children that what we know, works.
That the forces larger than comprehension do not
after all, threaten it but, like parents,

are subject too; like science, susceptible
to miracles in its infancy. Here was one:
the battened grass, the woman in the wall,
the breast, the child, the hospitality of stone.

Why they walled her up seems academic.
They have their reasons. She was a woman
with a nursing child. Walled she was
and dying. But even when they surmised

there was nothing of her left but dust and ghost
at dawn, at dusk, at intervals
the breast recalled, wilful as the awe
that would govern village lives, her milk flowed.

And her child suckled at the wall, drew
the sweetness from the stone and grew
till the cracks knew only wind and weeds
and she was weaned. Centuries ago.

THE CELLAR

I have left a light on the carpet's whorl.
Still as cobweb, batwing, breath, I am large
as an ogre on the stair. Larger still,
the forms I know are there: moving, sleeping,
parting in the afternoons each other's
hair. Do not think I have ever found
a thighbone or a crusted bowl to bridge
those yester-leavings with today's. There is
nothing but the smell of fear to tell me
they are near me in the dark.

                Padding down
the stair, the walls I scrabble in thin air
my elbows hooked, my fingers webbed, it seems
I visit on occasion. Occasions
flow thick and fast as snowflakes. I conjure
shapes that bare their teeth in water, mouthing
prophecies. In the tree, the monkey-mask
laughs across savannahs as he tells me
his people will survive.

                Closer, I seek
my mother's amulet. She is engrossed.
Her youngest is a girl, born with a growl.
Now I am here, I shall make friends with her.
It is not too late. While there is a lull
in the shooting from the woods, I shall make
the most of it: teach her to speak, watch her
gambol with her cousins in the clearing.

When she stops to sniff the air, clean of man,
herb on the wind will remind her of her
mother frowning in the steam from the pot.
In her sleep she will learn to roll away
from dripping leaves; keep dry in all monsoons.
And she will dream of the great uprising.

A ring of eyes. In every pair of eyes
a forest fire. On every upturned face
a wash of sundown layered on the rock.
She scans the smoke. Where is her mother's face?
Among her brothers, her own two sisters?
Where? Even elders in the outer ring
have shed their stoop. Grandmothers are yearlings
in the crowd. Cousins she has known from birth
are lost to her. She sees no name, no age,
no landscape of a life on any face,
no self she knows.

          But the marrow burning
in their bones races, fuels up, upwards
to her face. The youngest is the tallest.
The apex of the pyre. And through the sex
of every man and beast whose face is razed
by flame her rage is fed. And she will raise
her arms, place her palms flat on the belly
of the ceiling and as the crescendo
of their roar plumbs the plenum beyond sound
to a vision of the core, letting rip
the gag of generations...
                        she will push.

John Rety

MEMO: PLEASE LOOK INTO THIS

It was a good day at his office
except for the leather seat of his revolving chair
which was too hot for his buttocks.
His secretary was careless about the blinds
and the sun's rays were allowed to sit
on *his* seat, warming his seat,
before his seat sat on the seat
of his revolving chair.
On the partners' desk lay the agreement.
He held the judge's consent
in his chubby hands,
not one comma, not one dot needs to be altered.
The room was now cool, he drew the blinds himself,
just one soft light shining
on the all important documents.
The heat of the seat now only
bothered him as a passing irritation.
The deal was duly signed.
Seventy square acres of streets and tenements
were to be demolished:
They were due to be renewed long ago.

The tenants will not like it a bit,
but once the judgment has been given,
the rest was a mere formality –
what were solicitors, bailiffs
and the police for anyway?
Shelters and hospitals
will take care of the rest.

It may take a little time,
but just look at the town
say twenty years from now.
It will be his favourite town.
Oh, he loved the colour brown!
Victory over the poor now made him magnanimous,
he told his secretary over the intercom
that she may go home.
Then when all was quiet he carefully
opened the secret drawer where he kept
his sandwiches. He ate slowly,
privately and with the same determination
that he brought to bear on all his business dealings.
I have not seen him since.
Possibly he died.
There is no way of finding out.
The town isn't there any more.

1986

DECLARATION

I was one of them and they'd left me behind,
for time was their own and they had little space.
Now they are as far away in time as in space.
What was it they had objected to?
Perhaps they were as sorry as I am today,
for let me not pretend, I do miss them still,
although they were so cruel to me.
Your time will come, they yawned, but it is not yet.
I poked at the fire while they snored in bed.
They were polite, icily polite,
the Great Ones at whose feet I sat.
How many days and nights have I sacrificed
just to be near them!
But if I had been blind or deaf
or bereft of brains
without a sense of smell or touch,
it would have been the same.
They were great just seconds before I had entered the room,
as trembling legs took me upstairs to their presence,
had I but tiptoed
so that they could not sense my approach
so that I could have observed them as they really were,
but no, I never saw their greatness at all.
I saw blood, I saw love, I saw drunken stupor.
That's all I saw.

1985

Patrick Fetherston

WANTING

Some lack in one.
What you didn't do,
thought you ought
to have done,
to have stolen back
the merest
self-liking with;
for with the lack
simply of
self-liking, I,
if I were you,
would start to crack.

BRANWELL BRONTË

In his portrait of the three
Charlotte's the one with the reality
and the holdfast look, Emily's
an interrogatory ghost, and Anne
might be taking part in an ambush
in a bad dream.

In his
father's bedroom there weren't
many mansions: *they*
were provided by Angria,
by the convivial 'admiration'
of the villagers, by drink, by dope.

You daubed and prosed, got your seed
ripened by a real lady, lost jobs,
went reeling off into epilepsy.

But Charlotte remained
the accomplice/governess.
With Emily closer to you
generically, both of you
at one time animators,
all your short lives animists.

AN INSTANT OF DEPRIVATION

You were becoming acquainted
with the living strength
(light's continual (love's)
new-to-me losing-me (losing-*you*)
much-shifting cunning break)
of many a thing I, hidden
in the world, when
politic, would lose.

THE ANSWER IS A VERY OLD FLAGSTONE

Ever since I was dressed
and laid down
I have been kissed
on the face
by rubber and leather – even by skin.

Through the last two I have
conducted lightning
once in a way – when long-lying
heels replaced
ordinary transient soles.

But now I am trite,
my support and earthing alike
ignored by the contingent.

Roselyn Walter

WORDS

She thought
words would slow down
lick into shape
noise in her head
grief in her gut.
Give to them substance,
give to them name.

She hoped
feelings of loss
would dissolve, disappear
as the agony poured
in spate out of her.
Comfort would come
from somewhere, from someone.

She feared
  endless repeats
    of this pain
      on
          and
              on.

RIVULET

An odd fly
burrs by.
A smile of sunlight
cracks
across the scowl
of shade.

All else is still
but for the sound
that penetrates increasingly
as smoothness shatters on rough stone
and bubbles gurgle quietly.

Awareness comes
quite suddenly
of yet another depth below
reflecting unexpectedly
a filigree of branch and sky.

Why is it
tongue can savour smells
that nostrils taste, so easily
when blunted eyes refuse to hear
what ears see with such clarity?

Valerie Chazan

WATERWAYS

Along the margins of the wash
the heron stalk-standing and silent
shrouded in dark, waits.
Unlike drains we know, closed, concealed,
these are vast waterways criss-crossing
the fens. You have to be quick
to see the life that fills this open countryside.

Rainbows here stretch from beginning to end.
Woolly bands of cloud in blue marbled sky
extend as far as the eye can see.
The feel of loneliness, the space, few trees
to warm the view. Homes askew with subsidence
tilt toward the the river flow – straight straight.

On to mighty Denver Sluice. The different
levels leave us muddled and confused.
The sameness of this Anglian world
so carefully drained and built by man.
We are lost amongst the tall whispering grasses,
and the endless banks you have to climb
to see the River Ouse high above you.

Dinah Livingstone

THIRST

My body mostly water
now I remember that stream
Exmoor red bed boulders
intervals in its falling music
filling my Camden ears
locked limbs to flow with it
and oh, to heal my heart
whose systole/diastole
these two loved places are
in Britain – one pastoral
retreat, the sacred wood,
renewal baptism,
the other dusty familiar
full of faces
meeting of possibility
for pillars of gold metamorphosis,
speaking to each other
the beautiful city.
And the rain falls
on the just and the unjust
in its bounty.

No, the land is cursed,
the body politic
despised and neglected.
Now that soft grey cloud
the common good
becomes the start of a billion pound
production line. It is sold
as well as our soil, minerals,
energy, skills, telecommunications,
for private profit called
plc but cynically
not for the public.
Citizens queue at standpipes
for what they fear is contaminated.
The very act of selling it
already slips in poison
and our bodies mostly
built of it. Sold. Fools' gold.
Unhope. Land of my heart
we are unclean, we stink.
What skylark water will wash our body?
Sweet heaven
what shall we drink?

AT THE GATES

Where are the gates of hell?
Through Ludgate, Aldgate, Bishopsgate
and others all now notional
enter the world financial centre,
where natty youngish men,
eternally thirty one,
poplin shirted, worsted suited –
only the best, having commuted
daily from costly little gems
somewhere near longitude zero –
yup an English that yoyos
between yawn and snakebite,
crouch in worship of mammon's angels;
green-eyed mechanical networkers
post over land and ocean without rest,
while these acolytes only
stand and wait for profit,
hum its hymns
here in their temple.

In this service they buy and sell
anything at all, agony,
pain, degradation, remote
and perfectly willing to cancel
a village, a jungle, a people
just for the hell of it.

Deleted, cut from the file,
to these gates descended word,
called gospel
(bad news for the rich),
whose challenge rang through that hall
(Shift lock!):
THOU ART DOCTOR OF DEATH, DRINK THAT THOU MADEST.
I THAT AM LORD OF LIFE, LOVE IS MY DRINK
AND FOR THAT DRINK TODAY I DIED UPON EARTH.

And this voice rises again.
('Well really, now the great unwashed
not only smell but screech!')
Even now in this London
winter, ten years on
from that vicious abuse of poor Francis
on the threshold of number ten,
word rises again.

Kathleen McPhilemy

THE MOTHERS' LAMENT FOR THE DEATH OF CUCHULLAIN

They're wild bitter the Billy Boys
they'll not concede
a hand's span to the hag-haunted
land of the south.

Bitter indeed the Billy Boys
scourging western Maeve;
they burned out her steeples and forests
purged her of cattle and pride.

Wild indeed are the Billy Boys
who killed their father, the king
and their only sons, begotten
of rape not love.

They're wild bitter the Billy Boys
hounds of northern Cuchullain
sons, though not of his body
who loved not women.

        Some say he rode a black horse.
        Some say he rode a white horse.
        All know his iron shoe
        scarred the land from corner to corner.

        Black Will on the corner gable
        sword aloft like a salmon leaping;
        but a fish needs water
        a man needs sons and women.

They're wild bitter the Billy Boys
bitter inheritance Cuchullain willed them;
red-eyed, long-toothed, wild and gorgeous
Cuchullain, mad dog of Ulster.

Wildly, bitterly the Billy Boys
career through the ages
fleeing from water, searing the earth
hot after fire.

And as they burn and are consumed
black-hooded hags
cackle and wail like the crackling flames
for their wild, bitter Billy Boys.

MY FORMIDABLE GREAT AUNT

Mad old women earn the right to rage,
jib, baulk, stalk away high-hat;
so praise the awkward ones, who talk too loud
who come in late and hog the centre stage;
my great aunt's like that.

My great aunt is the goddess of our hearth
and, like some lesser oracle she squats
over our memory, reveals our tribal past;
a necessary presence, she binds us in
demands our duty.

My great aunt is outrageous, did go mad
at a difficult age. For great aunt every age
was difficult; she met them all head-on.
A frog-princess, she battled through her life
with graceless courage.

So praise my great aunt, last of the high bourgeois
my spinster great aunt, defiantly a miss.
Art school, India and then she lived alone
in a gingerbread house. She rose at noon
breakfasted off old newspapers.

My great aunt lived on art's perimeter
and at the edge where family finds its centre.
She painted a little; she never married.
I could have been like her, but lack her strength
or else was luckier.

She is amazing; not like that mad old witch
the Polish singer near the children's school
who rants in mittel-European, sprays
the street with rage. My great aunt's not like that.
She is not like that.

AMNESIA

The lady has been away
for five years or more, her absence
has not been noticed;
she returns to a body that is older
and worse, her eyesight
prime and precious instrument
is not what it was.

Some things have stayed the same:
books paper pencil pen
still there, a little dusty.
Some things have changed:
she meets the children;
they are, of course, enchanting.

She brings no souvenirs,
she has no traveller's tales;
from those who do enquire
her answers slide away;
her gaze is glazed, opaque,
as dumb as absence.

JOY

God might be a name for what is missing
this darkness in the house. In the hard light
of the street, selves jostle; children
hunch, heads down, from the school gate
into a new cold. But a little money
coats her in her half life. Furred
with indifference, she says: 'In my new place
I'll line the walls from roof to floor
with Hockneys, and have no need of windows.'

For it's the possibility of joy that terrifies her;
merciless as the moon, a white light
finds out her furthest, coldest corners,
the fearful caution of her self-regard
the mean economies she's made of love.
But as she huddles in head-banging misery
beneath the ricochet of searching beams
perhaps she learns the size of emptiness
the want of love, the want of joy there is.

NAWROZ: KURDISH NEW YEAR 21.3.1985

This day was spring's beginning:
no promises, under these skies.
Only bleached faces, pale as daffodils
that children left too long beneath the stairs
struggle to light. There are no buttonholes
and gallantry's unstiffened by the damp.
Only the peeling miners' badges
still boast a kind of honour.

The honour's in the loyalty to time
actual days and dates, not the turning seasons.
This spring the sly buds mock us: our banners sink.
As New Year greens the marchers drift away.
Though every tree has borne its megaphone
and we stand knee-high in leaflets, there are no words
to carry home. How dumb we have become
our silence is our guilt, the treachery of clerks.

The difficulty's in honouring the truth:
to match the shifting inner outer worlds
to find the words, transgress what friends expect.
We need a language as subtle-sour as tears
that stung to see the miners sent ahead
defeated banner high, to lead the Londoners;
how cheap the cheer we gave, as we resigned them
to the sad safe storage of history.

This spring belongs to refugees and miners
to Kurds who celebrate in a new language
their own story of Azdahak and Kawa
an end of tyranny, a hope of freedom.
Words come round again; the letter comes
that orders deportation. Very subtle now
in all the shades of their defilement
the words are ours and witness to the time.

PERFORMANCE

'The horse and the rider are one,'
said the flat-capped countryman
who stood by the unpainted rail
of the jumping enclosure.

Lines in parallel
boy's back and horse's
as they rose in a perfect arc
to the triple bars.

That achieved perfection
celebrates itself
and is a moment's celebration
in the watcher's eye:

we are borne up in communion
by a horse, by a song.

Peter Campbell

AS THE HAZEL BURNS

Never place the last piece
in a jigsaw
that's the Devil's job.
Don't count out
all the chimes at midnight
that's when the clock will stop.

A hawk is always more than a hawk
a legend in the steely sky
till you dissect his nature
on the cold frozen ground
and the light has gone out of its eye.

No man is ever less than a man
when he greets the world with fear
when he lays in driftwood for winter
or watches the dawn draw near.

A circle was never meant to be drawn
for the two ends meld like rock.
Never close the lid of a perfect dream
that you cannot yet unlock.

Remember the scree-scarred mountain
that overlooked your birth.
Remember the sinewy roots of hawthorn
and the cool crumbled taste of earth.

The snows will still fall
after you die
and the dragonfly arise.
Seek not your own perfection
on that hearth madness lies.

HEALTH ACT

Hold me.
Hold me.
Hold me – cries the girl.
The girl in hospital clothes.
She kneels on tat carpet squares,
knuckles the joins,
rocks against the orange armchair,
pressing her forehead into the Texturene.
Hold me. Hold me – she cries.
And turn that fucking television off.

The evening team are moving back out.
(They have sat in the sluices
watching their clocks pass eight.)
Coolly they edge the room,
reading their newspapers upside-down,
drift near the window curtains
counting, counting, checking the back way out.
Hold me. Hold me. Hold me.
They gather round neatly,
finger their cuffs in unison.

When will the slap come?
When will the blanket be brought?
Evans is Jesus.
Evans is the bastard –
coming from the nursing station
with his blue suit still on.

Every sympathy in order.
They take her to the treatment room,
they take her to seclusion.
Beyond harm's reach.
And just in time to enter on the shift report.

At twenty past nine we'll make ourselves toast
and cluster in the servery.
We were the ones with the power to hold,
the power to make safe the danger.
We cannot act through want of health –
angling for leave under Section Three,
dreaming of mealtimes outside Saint David's.
We are the ones with the holding power.
Evans is our saver.
Evans is the bastard.

FOURTH STATION

Cricklewood Station,
Cricklewood Station.
I wait for the five o'clock
with resignation.
It's down to Kings Cross
for a conversation
with a man in a bookshop
creased with perspiration.

I've never seen the colours over west so hard,
like ripples of blackcurrant on a faded postcard.
No coronas on the floodlights in the marshalling yard.
It's the kind of night God must have used
for passing on the word.

Graffiti on the shelters,
on Cricklewood Station,
chalking the genetic code
of mass imagination,
putting out the candles
of a deeper indignation,
jumping on the five o'clock
for a private assignation.

I've never heard such singing of the voltage in the wire,
like the suicidal pleadings of a tabernacle choir.
They can keep you out of work, they can't put out the fire.
It's the kind of night God must have used
to push sexual desire.

Graffiti say that God was here
on Cricklewood Station.
If I had known it soon enough
I would have booked a conversation
to offer to that great divine
heartfelt congratulation
for leaving us a night like this
in form of compensation.

I've never seen the moisture on the brick so sheer,
like ear-rings that are clinging to a deaf mute's ear.
There's a cutting kind of silence in this section of the year.
It's the kind of night God must have used
to make his passion clear.

Cricklewood Station,
Cricklewood Station,
I wait for the five o'clock
with indignation.
It's down to Kings Cross
for a brief flirtation.
And the evening in the back row
of a godless generation.

VIDEO WAR

Johnny, go down to the video war.
Rejoice says your country's leader.
There's work to be done on Falklands moor
and your own town cannot need you.

Take care for your Mum, take care for yourself,
take pride in your Queen and country.
There's nothing here for a man with a bairn
when he's unemployed and thirty.

It's Super Mouse on the box tonight
and it's Joker and Gipsy Bojangles.
When our heroes go in on the box tonight
look out for the camera angles.

Johnny, I cried when you sailed out that day
though I knew that your going was needed,
but the shot of your grave on the tv last night
will live on when the pride has receded.

Take care for your Mum when she visits that moor.
Do no ask me for pain and for pity.
I get it each evening, six days of the week
when I'm doing the wee lad's knitting.

It's Bojangles on the news tonight
and Joker and red Super Mouse.
When our heroes go in on the box tonight
I'll not be in the house.

I'll be alone.

THE PAIN OF LOVE

For Lorraine

The pain of love is terrible.
Coasters slip in unseen
before the hoot of dawn.
They weigh against the knuckled piers,
oily water lisps at their sides,
and seagulls eat the cake.
The pain of love bites like an early squall.

The pleasure of love is terrible.
We untie the world.
Bookham, Egham and Dorking fields –
they are listed with Barbary.
Poppies snag the nearest corn,
the rooks wheel down.
The pleasure of love bites like harvest mice.

The pain of love is terrible.
Why should he die and be lost to my touch?
Only in agony now do I watch him.
Only the deathless tie
linking us between the eyes.
Only that heart which cannot stop
– nor can ever be made to.
The pain of love bites like a benison.

Brian Docherty

HARLEQUIN AND JULIET

Friday night tv turns insult painful
so in a bid to stop his brain
clacking like a deranged teleprinter,
he reports to the pub for an anaesthetic.
Bass, and rum chasers go down well,
all his friends have new stories
but as he relaxes into their mood,
his social immunity expires at first sight
and old feelings dance through him
like a column of fire.
His workings are freewheeling wildly
as the woman who has reactivated him
glides her grace and beauty barwards.
Tracking her in the mirror, he follows
and when she grants him an audience,
he has trouble saying anything sensible,
left feeling he's in the wrong play.

CUTS IN THE WELFARE STATE

Italian dreams dissolve into the background static
of a different day in the same England,
as rain registers gray upon grey,
coffee helping me play Hunt the Braincell,
reading the misinformation in the Daily Blag
about multiple attacks on my welfare state:
busfares 18% more highway robbery,
rates a new level of property speculation,
anaesthetic up fourpence a pint.

Today I'm summoned to the surgery run
by the Dept. of Harassment and Self Sufficiency
to deal with cancer of the wallet.
Passing the check-in desk my energy entropies
under the heavy hand organising my life;
when I join the queue for another chance
to practise the Old Ceremonial Grovel,
the waiting room resembles the airport terminal
of some Nazi-infiltrated banana republic.
I'd like a ticket for the parachute cabaret
on a plane to some faraway beach.

Eventually I'm called into a cubicle
to be told: We are trying to help you.
We don't like your ingratitude.
We have nice work if you want it –
a worthwhile function in Robot Junction
sweating to make the money tree grow.
You should relocate to the country,
perform headstands on the sewage farm.
You're not really ill! Cure yourself
or we'll amputate your benefit.

THE GREATEST VIOLENCE
IS SAYING GOODBYE

How long can we continue
this heartless struggle of denial
shredding each other like icebergs
each time our separated lives intersect?
You are like some submarine
running silent through arctic certainty
ignoring my incoherent desolation
making me feel like some
mushroom-primed Nordic psychopath
all blood-crusted beard and rusty axe
sent to provide sport for Loki
drowning in the deep dark
waters of the Carlingfjord
torpedoed by your personal politics.

Now I know the hardest word
like the shirt-tearing shieldbiters
who bade farewell to Thor
and embraced the White Christ
for a fat life of peaceful trade
with shaven Saxons and Rusland brothers.
I'd rather be deaf and dumb before
either of us utters that awful word
people use like an axe
to splinter love into separation.
Can't we find some sandy beach
meet under a midnight sun
make a new start like Aske and Embla
find a way to trust and love again?

THE LIZARDS OF POMPEII

When the green mountain was empty,
we were there;
when the Phoenicians and Romans came,
we observed their arrival;
when the Romans started building,
they made for us dark corners;
when the lava came
we were there;
when their 'green mountain'
blossomed forth into an angry volcano,
we were there;
when the small eruptions came,
we died by the thousands;
when the great eruptions came,
we fried and roasted by the millions;
the Romans perished to a man,
some of us survived;
all through the long buried years,
we were there;
when the Bourbon king sent his excavators,
we saw them arrive;
when the tourists came on the Circumvesuviana,
we were there;
when they filed through the Porta Marina,
we observed them;
when the railway is twisted into rusty ruin,
we will be there;
when their towns are silent again,
we will remain.

SUNDAY CONCERT IN NOEL PARK

Our libretto recommends a joyful noise
on a day fit for penguins or skiers,
frosted like an Alpine Christmas;
the wind is tape-hiss from a recorder
saturated by a Salvation Army band
crashing out *Onward Christian Soldiers*,
competing with the body music playing
in recital rooms up and down our street.

We are in tune with our neighbours
exchanging French kisses like presents,
rehearsing our history of popular music
rolling from Africa's burundi beat
with its double heartbeat rhythm,
through a New Orleans piano boogie
in our best barrelhouse style,
to Kerry slides from Sliabh Luachra
in the old press and draw fashion;
and the bagpipes' octopus pantomime
till we don't know if we're playing
the pipes or the pipes are playing us.

And society is strobe-frozen by love,
the world of 'history' and 'events'
is a movie trapped between takes
until we roll off our rostrum,
stumble down the stairs for breakfast
in time with the beat of the street;
all members of the same orchestra
playing variations of a very old tune,
waiting for our conductor to return
and hold auditions for the House Band.

EPILOGUE

By the Editor

CHORUS

Now suddenly our time on earth seems short,
another London spring excites the air.
Street children gallop on the grass and shout,
trust thrusting freer from their mothers' care.
A blessing on fresh couples in the park,
unconquered sun strokes even stiff old bones.
Joy stirs, disturbs once more before the dark:
I am it all, heart hurts, sheer pleasure groans.
The utterable ground of love is this:
it matters how we are and what we do,
adore all flesh knowing all flesh is grass,
the mystery is you; and you; and you.
Quick quality of detail is the thing
that marks the common time in which we sing.

ABOUT THE AUTHORS

Alison Islin lives in Edgware. She is married with a boy of 3 and expecting another baby in February. Worked in magazines and newspapers for nine years and has had fiction and articles published.
Andrew Woodward is a freelance broadcaster and adult literacy tutor.
Beate Lux Smeed came to England in 1936 as a child refugee from Hitler Germany. Trained as a medical photographer and worked in various hospitals here and abroad. Now works for war-blinded physiotherapists.
Betty Wall: Born in Bridport Dorset in 1925. Studied at the Slade. Interested in art, nature, ecclesiastical embroidery and trying to keep afloat.
Bob Rodgers was born in 1922 in Thornton Heath. 'Early recollections: stood in the street with family and neighbours to see the R101 airship off on its last flight. A few years later, now moved to Addiscombe, stood in the street with family and neighbours to watch the Old Crystal Palace burn down. In between those two events my father lost his business in the depression, made many moves and ended up in the Workhouse. I had no schooling till I was about 12½, served in Royal Navy during the war. My ship mate Paul was a great help, from him I learned how to use a dictionary as I was unable to spell and could only read the smaller words. I started to write poetry and short stories for fun in 1943. I joined Dinah's group in 1985, then I frequented poetry gigs at the Troubadour Cafe Brompton Road and the Wooden Lambs Chiswick.'
Brian Docherty was born in Glasgow in 1953 and came to London in 1974. He is a Ph.D. student at Essex University, writing a thesis on the Beat Poets. He is a founder member of the Lumiere Co-op Press. He co-edited *Insights into Nineteenth Century Suspense* (Macmillan 1988), edited *Insights into American Crime Fiction* (Macmillan 1988), *Insights into American Horror Fiction* (Macmillan 1989), and is currently editing other titles.
Bryan Abraham is a freelance editor and proof reader and lives in North London.
Christopher Truman was born in Malaysia in 1954, went to school in England and currently runs an export-oriented company making pollution control systems.
Cicely Herbert is tutor in charge at Camden Institute Holmes Road Branch. With Ann Langton she wrote *87 Holmes Road* (1989). A Barrow Poet and founder member of Poems on the Underground. She has written several performance pieces with music by Jim Parker: *Petticoat Lane* (BBC tv), *Monster City* and *A Dog's Life* (for the Cockpit Theatre), *Scenes from Victorian London* and *La Comédie Humaine* (for the Nash Ensemble).
David Schiff is a university lecturer, veteran runner and father of two children.
Dennis Simmons 'was found lurking in a bed at the village of Mereworth (Kent) in 1938. Since then lots of people have tried to force me to remove from between the sheets mostly unsuccessfully. Came to London to live, 1961. Resident in Swiss Cottage since 1964. Have had a few 'minor scraps' published – as all good boxing lovers should. A cartoon lover.'

About the Authors

Dinah Livingstone has run the Camden Voices group since 1978. Her most recent collection is *Keeping Heart* Poems 1967-89 (Katabasis 1989).

Donie Dempsey: Ireland's first poet in residence in a secondary school. Broadcast on radio and tv. Published *Cabbage Plants aren't Weeds* (1979).

Elen N.A. Read: 'I have been writing verse since my school days, but having been ridiculed and ignored through it have retained a reticent and sensitive attitude in acknowledging it, in fact have been hiding my efforts. I feel I must thank you for encouraging me to bring out my efforts in the open. I have been introduced to the classical poets when, being thin, white and delicate at school I was not allowed to join in the classes' physical exercises or gymnastics, so sitting it out, to fill in the time, I began to read poetry and tried to learn poems by heart. I was born, bread and buttered happily in London and in my teen years frequented the Old Vic where I paid 6d in the Gallery.'

Elizabeth Trew is a South African living in London. She teaches English as a Second Language at Camden Institute.

Francesca Reynolds has worked for Friends of the Earth, Women's Environmental Network and now works in a graphic design studio. Published two collections *Unbidden Guest* (1986) and *Nobody Special* (1988).

Francis Oeser grew up in Australia and now lives and works locally. He married an Australian potter and they have three children. Poetry published: *Black Notes* (1983), *Seasons End* (1984), *Africa Sung* (1987) and *Baybreak* (due 1990).

Helen Barrett lives with an adopted cat in a co-op flat. She has always worked with and periodically carried out research on people, her current preoccupation being the experience of childminders' and childminded children.

Jane Duran was born in Cuba and grew up in the USA. Her poems have appeared in *London Magazine*, *Ambit* and two Arts Council anthologies. Her poem 'Boogie Woogie' won the judges' second prize in the TLS/Cheltenham Festival Competition in 1987.

Jeni 'has been and will be writing for ever. In 1985 she won a GLC poetry prize.'

Jill Bamber trained as an occupational therapist and has worked in psychiatric hospitals. Married with two sons. Began writing poetry in 1978 and has recently given up working as an OT to concentrate on writing and painting.

John Cook is a painter and engraver. Studied at the R.A. Schools, taught at Edinburgh College of Art. Now retired from teaching he is living and working in Camden Town. He published a limited edition of a book of poems *Aftermath* illustrated with his wood engravings in 1986.

John Jolliffe is working as a psychotherapist and advocate in self-analysis. He was a founder member of Asclepion, a free style therapeutic community in London.

John Rety was editor of *Freedom* in the sixties. He currently runs the Torriano Meeting House. Published *A Song of Anarchy* (Box 2, 1989).

Katherine Gallagher is an Australian resident in London since 1979. Her poems have been published widely in Australia and the UK. She has four collections, including *Passengers to the City* (Hale and Iremonger, Sydney 1985) and most recently, *Fish-Rings on Water* (Forest Books, London 1989).

Kathleen McPhilemy grew up in Belfast, lived in London till recently but has now moved to Oxfordshire. She is married with four children. She has published *Fat Dad* (1983); *Dulse and Yellow Man* (Hearing Eye 1988) and *Witness to Magic* (Hearing Eye 1989).

Mary Mohan was born in Co. Monaghan, Eire in 1949 and has lived in Camden Town since 1965. Her short stories have appeared in Fontana and Pan anthologies and her poetry has been published in Beehive Press anthologies and in *Envoi*.

Mimi Khalvati was born in Iran and now lives in Highgate with her two children. A selection of her poems is forthcoming in an anthology of 'New Voices' from Anvil in 1990.

Myra Schneider: Her most recent poetry collection was *Cathedral of Birds* (Littlewood Press 1988). Her second collection, *Cat Therapy* was reprinted in 1989. She has published a novel for children, two for teenagers and an adult novel but her main writing interest now is poetry. A new collection is due in 1991. She teaches multi-handicapped adults part time at a day centre, runs writing workshop classes, one-off sessions and gives talks and readings all over the country.

Patrick Fetherston was born at Rotherfield in 1928 and has lived in London since 1950. He received an Arts Council Writer's Award in 1969 and has published 13 volumes of poetry and prose, including *The World was a Bubble* (Burning Deck 1979), *The Natural History of Another Country* (poetry: 1986); *Stories* (1987) and *Muses Awaited* (fiction: 1988).

Peter Campbell lives in Cricklewood. He was born in Strathtay in the Scottish Highlands and came to London in 1973. He was a founder member and the first secretary of Survivors Speak Out, a national organisation promoting action by recipients of mental health services. Among his published writings are two collections of poems: *In Two Countries* (1984) and *The Way it Feels* (1986). A third, *A Breath Outwards* is in preparation. He is a supporter of Hendon Football Club.

Richard Armstrong is 30 and currently a civil survant. He hopes to write full time in the long term.

Roselyn Walter, a musician, started writing poetry during the short terminal illness of an old friend two and a half years ago.

Shelah Florey: 'Born in Somerset and aiming to get back ever since. I've lived in London for more than sixty years. I began writing poetry after retiring.'

Steve Doyle is from Bolton Lancs. He came to London in 1977 and has worked mainly on building sites. He lived in Camden but now he lives in Waterloo.

Susan Jankowski: Cumbrian (exiled), mother of three children.

Tim Sanders lived in Kentish Town for ten years but recently moved to Bucks with his wife and daughter.

Valerie Chazan lives in North London and runs a floating restaurant in Docklands.

Veronica Cohen: 51 very soon. Married to a GP. Two daughters. Hobbies apart from writing: Art History, playing the flute and piano.

Zanna Beswick is a television drama script editor and producer. She prefers to write full time when circumstances allow. Her poems have been published in various magazines and anthologies, including *Resurgence* and *Writing Women*.

Zoë Bailey: Born 1930, has worked as an editor and writer for BBC schools Radio writing stories and poems for children. She has a 21 year old daughter.